crohnic

POEMS **JASON PURCELL**

crohnic

ARSENAL PULP PRESS
VANCOUVER

CROHNIC
Copyright © 2025 by Jason Purcell

All rights reserved. No part of this book may be reproduced in any part by any means—graphic, electronic, or mechanical—without the prior written permission of the publisher, except by a reviewer, who may use brief excerpts in a review, or in the case of photocopying in Canada, a licence from Access Copyright.

ARSENAL PULP PRESS
Suite 202 – 211 East Georgia St.
Vancouver, BC V6A 1Z6
Canada
arsenalpulp.com

The publisher gratefully acknowledges the support of the Canada Council for the Arts and the British Columbia Arts Council for its publishing program and the Government of Canada and the Government of British Columbia (through the Book Publishing Tax Credit Program) for its publishing activities.

Arsenal Pulp Press acknowledges the xʷməθkʷəy̓əm (Musqueam), Sḵwx̱wú7mesh (Squamish), and səlilwətaɬ (Tsleil-Waututh) Nations, custodians of the traditional, ancestral, and unceded territories where our office is located. We pay respect to their histories, traditions, and continuous living cultures and commit to accountability, respectful relations, and friendship.

Arsenal Pulp Press is committed to reducing the consumption of non-renewable resources in the making of our books wherever possible. We make every effort to use materials that support a sustainable future. This book is printed on paper made with 100 percent sustainable recycled fibre content.

Cover and text design by Jazmin Welch
Cover art by Mathew Thomson
Edited by Jordan Abel
Copy-edited by Catharine Chen
Proofread by Alison Strobel

Printed and bound in Canada

Library and Archives Canada Cataloguing in Publication:
Title: Crohnic : poems / Jason Purcell.
Names: Purcell, Jason, author
Identifiers: Canadiana (print) 20250144875 | Canadiana (ebook) 20250144891 |
    ISBN 9781834050102 (softcover) | ISBN 9781834050119 (EPUB)
Subjects: LCGFT: Poetry.
Classification: LCC PS8631.U7338 C76 2025 | DDC C811/.6—dc23

Somewhere there is an unbroken
wall of light scraping
over the surface of the earth
—Jordan Abel

I was in the underworld
Down in my guts
—Erin Robinsong

On the banks of the North Saskatchewan I shed
my velvet having to rest again on the white powder

line snow like a tablet crushed and blown toward the crisp
blank future a shrinking

place where health and death are the same
temperature where I am calculated and reduced so

there is less of me to keep alive on the banks
of the North Saskatchewan I sat down and sacrificed

Lindsay gives me the idea for this book.

Lindsay is a nurse who cares for patients who, like me, take medications that make one sicker to make one better. It's a hard thing to handle, she says. A lot of people struggle.

While writing this book I have been visited by side effects: I have vomited, bled, grown dizzy and weak, fatigued and cold. My face has swollen, my hair has grown brittle. My sleep has been dashed backward: I sleep early and wake naturally and alert long before sunrise. My skin thins, grows more vulnerable. There is still pain but now it is a type called "manageable."

To help me live with a severe and long-undiagnosed case of Crohn's disease, each day I swallow down pills and every month I receive infusions by IV that whittle me down but keep me going in the meantime. Like Lindsay says, intense and persistent medical intervention can feel hard to handle.

But all the while, outside my window, winter goes on, teaching me how to rest. From my apartment perched in the trees of amiskwacîwâskahikan where I convalesce, where I look out onto the North Saskatchewan and her river valley, I learn how to wait. The trees lining the water lose their bulk and stand thin at the banks. The river freezes over with psoriatic plaque. Animals burrow, storing and hunting, knowing not to expend. Outside the city bogs and muskeg bubble, cradling that which slowly decomposes. Winter breathes slowly in sacred dormancy.

I am trying to learn an obvious lesson: everything is entangled in a relationship with life and death. Decay feeds life, and the non-human world does not seem to enforce strict division between these orders; life and death are both a kind of flourishing, co-creating possibilities. Winter puts us to sleep so we can be reborn. I take my prescribed and measured harms so that I can live more fully. The river flows, sheets over, changes state, and then .

freezes my body's dogged swelling
poisons me just the right amount another handful

a sprinkling of bleach discs to thin the bones thin
the skin keep my body quiet

this frozen place walking its wasted crystal
length less and less with each step rattling

through grey air from a body full of that which hurts
it to help it more shadow than anything else thin as trees

as sharp shuddering in the long winter of managed landscape
on the banks of the North Saskatchewan I am too

human and I impose that on everything that isn't too
clear-cut what ill-suited gaze did I carry down and fix

on this landscape its residents the narcissism of being
damaged and thinking the rest is too

a prescribing cold reaches toward and embraces
me the silver skin lifts and peels from the birch

at my side mosses turn their slow growth north
an animal leaves its fur in the branches.

It is why we have been given two
hands to hold in each
the dust that falls from the word
in any direction even when it is dry
toxin or cure all things
are poison all things are
exchange you may be
handed something else something
minacious that senses
the warmth in you and so winds
itself up the wrist squeezing reminding
you that to intervene is to bargain.

In the hospital's heights a nuthatch
on the atrium's topmost bridge hopping

tentatively and then seemingly frightened
by the rattling bed passing us takes flight

up to the glass above
I lose it in the trapped sun.

                    Down below are tiers
                    of potted trees presumably insects

                    who have been brought along
                    and are making do.

In the green
plastic sleeve I am told to safeguard

the medical reports and discharge forms
of which I am the subject

but not author until now
I write in the margins of documents

interventions to make them human
animal plant it is a living

document aren't I?

Medical Laboratory Report | *ALBERTA PRECISION LABORATORIES*

Report for: Purcell, Jason

In my dreams the creek
swells under the ice
that Zach and I stepped on once

he offered me his arm held
my footing his laugh filled
the basket the branches that hold bare

the sky in his hands my body
not so strong this place
on the walk back a bird

a delicate thing
its neck in all directions
its guts

The dripping sounds of fentanyl the sleepy
curling midazolam in the hollows
of my teeth the largest ulceration
2 centimetres long segment
extending beyond the eye
of the colonoscope patient
will be admitted to hospital
for IV steroids and pre-biologic workup.[1]

---

[1] Alberta Health Services, "Purcell, Jason, Endoscopy Procedure Report—External," January 3, 2023.

In 1661, *admitted* began to mean "allowed or enabled to enter; received or accepted into a place, organization, etc."[2] I wake up cold in a hallway I cannot look down with a grey curtain at my side and am told I am not yet able to go home. I require monitoring. I am allowed to enter a place of care. I am being received into the beeping linoleum structure. After years of dismissal, I am finally offered a diagnosis, membership within an order of disease. I prefer the second sense of the word: "accepted or recognized as true or valid; acknowledged as such by general assent or by admission of the speaker or writer."[3]

On the other side of the hospital it is winter.

---

[2] *Oxford English Dictionary*, "Admitted (adj.), sense 3," accessed October 24, 2024, https://doi.org/10.1093/OED/9269395748.
[3] *Oxford English Dictionary*, "Admitted (adj.), sense 2," accessed October 24, 2024, https://doi.org/10.1093/OED/5495780024.

Extensive active inflammatory bowel disease affecting much of the ileum, with signs of transmural penetrating diseases resulting in a phlegmonous area in the central anterior mid abdomen, with central tethering of multiple adjacent disease segments.[4]

Winter slowed to a treacle, crystal sap coating thick caverns of bark. Networks underground connecting one place to another, the bleating past to now.

I imagine the long fields of my gut dotted with tunnels, the body's sick efficiencies, making way for unrestricted movement for forms of life I have no dominion over.

---

4 Alberta Health Services, "Purcell, Jason, MR Enterography Study Result," January 5, 2023.

On the other side of the hospital the sore
wind the linoleum the unnoticeable shade

(though I tried to notice tried to recall the colour
as it felt against my bloodless feet its colourlessness

uneven could be tripped upon) from the denuded
window I see very little

beings small in their pairs the loping deer the rabbits
the winter furs the line of windows the distance

from my flickering beige room to the river
is not so great that the animals can't cross.

Severe, patchy granular and ulcerated mucosa with erosion in the terminal ileum, consistent with Crohn's disease; bleeding occurred after the intervention; performed four cold forceps biopsies.[5]

The hunter's dog bounds over the blue dome of snow, hollow mouthed but for the dangling ropes of gut. His bounty dragging behind him, wetting his fur, and my own knots longing to be longed for that way. His yapping fills me. The flapping curtain of my body breaks.

Multiple markedly thick-walled loops of small bowel are identified in the right quadrant and midline in the lower abdomen. This is associated with increased vascularity. The adjacent mesenteric fat demonstrates increased echogenicity consistent with inflammation. A small amount of free intraperitoneal fluid is demonstrated.[6]

Hemoglobin 111

MCV 80

CRP 142 mg/L

Here blankets are kept folded and warm, pelts that crawl with mites silver as buttons dancing in their pairs and that warm my animal skin.

---

5 Alberta Health Services, "Purcell, Jason, Endoscopy Procedure Report—External," January 3, 2023.
6 Alberta Health Services, "Purcell, Jason, US Pelvis Male," December 26, 2022.

    After waking I am moved

someone is called to roll me through the network

    of hallways and lifts

after making bids at small talk I recognize

    it is better to stay quiet and allow

all this to happen I shrink the architecture

    of this place loses shape

through each swinging doorway are spaces that grow

    increasingly muted

where light and sound are denser every place

    is liminal I don't want

to see or be seen but am deposited

    in a room where someone else

was hours ago plural or singular

    and left

with the light and noise that takes hours

and then I came to know the signs
evidence of lowbush blueberries

under the eyes dyeing
the small plain under each

Through the window the light leaks in
its own sound pinging like water
against the treed amber walls pill bottles

to the crowns of the Siberian larches yellow
erased in winter and soft the world in its capsule
isolated and artificial its murmuring vacant

white hundreds of acres of tile over
the floor that flattens the beetle and the hare
the felled trees erase an axis spinning

from the window the light from my eyes dapples
the details carved in the precious plastic: my name
dates that chart not progress but endurance

of that which fills the brittle walls rolling like snow
out of the bones hollowing the halls of my body
vulnerability to vulnerability so that I can remain

alight from the window *Larix sibirica* in its upward
gaze up like a flame my xylem
with drugs furiously up my wick

the steroids take
hold by reducing
permeability you are less

open doors within you
slam nothing but the crushing

creak of snow outside
your sleep blue falls you are kept
awake though an untranslatable

duration so hazy the air so cold
you can't see through it an opaque

sleeplessness mews at your eyetips
you are kept awake to witness
your slow-stitched healing

I miss the river.

    This room's window looks out into other windows pressed into beige flat exterior walls.

At home I can see the river from our living room window, such length of it. When I left for the hospital it was frozen and there was snow and ice covering it.

    Immediately upstream segment of small bowel is dilated at 4 centimetres, indicating functionally significant downstream stenosis. Approximately 30 centimetres upstream, there is further active disease, with approximately 5-centimetre segment of transmural penetrating disease, resulting in an ill-defined phlegmonous enhancing mass in the central anterior mesentery, with matting/tethering of several adjacent small bowel segments.[7]

---

[7] Alberta Health Services, "Purcell, Jason, MR Enterography Study Result," January 5, 2023.

That metaphor, the long ropes of guts a stream. Mine meander and divert, the muddy iron banks washing away, looping and merging into each other until I am a flooded mass, all the way up the boot.

Not far from here the river meets the creek. Down at the mouth are tooth marks in the soft wood. Their fibres, their strands, their wet mattedness. The animal fur. The beaver bring their microbiota to the trees.

A few centimetres further there is another lengthy segment (approximately 10 centimetres) of mural thickening with dilation of the immediately upstream segment.[8]

As it is freezing the river scales over. Flakes of ice with lifted edges form along its epidermis. In the dry cold it itches.

A further 10 to 15 centimetres upstream, there are two adjacent short segment skip lesions. These course over the superior aspect of the aforementioned phlegmonous area.[9]

The river meets the creek. Gradually the flows change. Obstacles are introduced, they meet elsewhere.

The inflamed gut struggles to absorb nutrients and those deficiencies manifest on the peeling skin. I separate the long layers and flip them like pages.

---

8 Alberta Health Services, "Purcell, Jason, MR Enterography Study Result," January 5, 2023.
9 Alberta Health Services, "Purcell, Jason, MR Enterography Study Result," January 5, 2023.

the beetles' paths overwritten the long fronds
of dill flattened the rows of cabbage and poppy
dots cleared away and the sick memories brown
the grooves underfoot in the hospital bed I unfurl
cabbage leaf by cabbage leaf the knowledges
I would like to tend to when I get out how to grow
how to preserve how to wend backward
in flight with the piping plover to reach
the time before our skin
was caked in dust and oil but kissed
by the lips of the poppy winding up
among the cabbage aphids in the greens
scented by the mustards nothing a weed
anymore nothing as unnatural as the white
plastic beneath our feet the thin
curtains between sick bodies washed
in the healthy rivers torn up used
now by nesting birds and small mammals
in their dens their bellies full of green
mottled with dew sparkling underwing

Getting down to the substance and feeling it all over the hands. Inside the hands. The saline flush used to ensure intravenous lines are closed systems free of air. To stave off irritation at the puncture site. In formulation the saline flush approximates the salt concentration of blood, just shy of a single percent of sodium chloride. Each time a bag is emptied into my veins—400 mg of hydrocortisone each day—my IV is flushed. Sometimes you can taste it, like you've put your mouth to the lips of the deep wet purple marsh and sucked in its cold.

Like black knot
tied and hanging from the branches

long ropes of tar that strangle
and atrophy.

When exposed to light the roots go orange. A burning dry peel of winter citrus out in the snow.

Extensive active inflammatory bowel disease affecting much of the ileum, with signs of transmural penetrating disease resulting in a phlegmonous area in the central anterior mid abdomen, with central tethering of multiple adjacent disease segments. As such, it is difficult to exclude inter-segment fistulization.[10]

Fistula: "an abnormal communication between two hollow organs … or between a hollow organ and the exterior."[11] Crohn's disease is cited as being one of the afflictions that coaxes these into formation, often between nearby bowel loops or between the bowel and adjacent organs. The word's first recorded use in 1382 is in reference to the *Cassia fistula*, a tree with "long, tubular pods,"[12] then takes on a musical resonance in 1398 describing pipe or reed instruments.[13] It obtains its medical definition in the fifteenth century when it begins to describe an "abnormal passage" between organs, cavities, and skin.[14]

Following myself upstream and then veering off course.

---

10 Alberta Health Services, "Purcell, Jason, MR Enterography Study Result," January 5, 2023.
11 *Oxford Concise Medical Dictionary* (9th edition), ed. Elizabeth Martin (Oxford University Press, 2015), under "fistula."
12 *Oxford English Dictionary*, "fistula (n.), sense 1," accessed September 21, 2024, https://doi.org/10.1093/OED/2842152206.
13 *Oxford English Dictionary*, "fistula (n.), sense 2," accessed September 21, 2024, https://doi.org/10.1093/OED/9062063791.
14 *Oxford English Dictionary*, "fistula (n.), sense 3a," accessed September 21, 2024, https://doi.org/10.1093/OED/8496127523.

Dwarf mistletoe interrupts the normal growth of the penetrated branch, sets off an inflammatory nerve, a seductive line of rheumatoid boughs. Called *witches' brooms*, these are "dense, broom-like clusters of proliferating branches or twigs" that "may be caused by infection with any of a number of organisms."[15]

The body finds a way around. The parasite burrows. Down below a snowshoe hare worries the giving bark. The lodgepole pine bleeds in all directions.

---

[15] *Oxford Dictionary of Plant Sciences* (4th edition), ed. Michael Allaby (Oxford University Press, 2019), under "witches' broom."

At week zero, we mark together the intervals, the nurses and I:
five minutes, ten, thirty, sixty, ninety, one hundred and twenty, that it takes for the bodies—human and animal—to meet.

Infliximab is an antibody designed to absorb the excess protein (tumour necrosis factor) that, in us, overpowers the body, firing up an inflammation response that damages the intestines. The medication is genetically engineered and combines two proteins: one from a human and one from a mouse. It is not completely human and so might look to the body as a threat to its defences. An allergic reaction to organic life is possible.[16]

In the winters they tunnel beneath the sun forging paths following their own wisdom.

---

16 Alberta Health Services, "Patient Information Sheet: Antibody to Tumour Necrosis Factor (Anti-TNF) (Biosimilar Infliximab) for Inflammatory Bowel Disease," February 6, 2017.

In the tall grasses the stacked logs
the buildings off the river the blossoms

the recombinant proteins harvested
from their shivering bodies seeking

warmth the common domains
health the untouched earth shelter

from the swooping hunters who take
in their blades the future and fly

with it together shaking in the earth
the scale of bodies stretches protects one

holds the other in its veins quaking with hope.

In the morning with my tray of food I am brought a small paper cup containing assorted pills: vitamins (the inflamed gut struggles to absorb vitamins and minerals; many patients are deficient in their unique ways), antibiotics, and this tiny yellow tablet the colour of a dull Easter chick. This one works as an immunosuppressant, another way of calming my body. I am to take it every day. In three to four months I will begin to recognize its effects.

This little pill called azathioprine that suppresses the blood cells, reducing inflammation. Vesica piscis. Its almond shape. Its seed.

In the coils of the MRI machine
that vibrate and bang against one another
I am comforted I am tethered
by an IV tucked under a warm blanket
restrained there are no expectations
of me other than to lie there to breathe
and not breathe in intervals the sound
mounts until it becomes visible and the rest
of the world ceases to exist anxiety
dissolves I am only my senses then
it ends and everything rushes back
into the cavity.

                Later my partner comes to visit and I am cold
                toward him I have never been able to say
                that I am scared I am never able
                to admit it I bristle I want
                to appear invulnerable it's the only way
                I know how to survive to say
                out loud that I am afraid and lonely and still
                have to stay here to endure
                would weaken me to admit
                    it would do nothing to get me out any sooner.

To stay here I have to lie feign a detachment
and stoicism a professional resolve so I do he looks
hurt and disappointed and leaves and I am alone looking
at myself until a nurse comes by to change
out another bag of hydrocortisone to keep me from feeling
I text him but the line is severed.

Getting down
into the muck of being
at times a person
I dislike I drag

through its sucking
rot the sodden leather
of my boot filling
with my shamed body

the distance goes queer
why go all that way after all
this why reach
for that spoiled horizon

where the waterlogged
flesh of black fruit hangs
in wisps and orbits round the still
insects nothing scatters

at the shot the future holds
does not react does not beckon
or welcome simply is
ugly and uncertain and violent

and the way toward it dark
shadowless this dose
keeps me here
with myself against

my own better judgment
my own instinct
the pills seeds
that germ like spite.

Every morning before breakfast and medication I am woken by the phlebotomist who takes his daily vials. Every day around lunchtime the results from my tests come in. I am waiting for my C-reactive protein levels to fall within the normal range. When I was admitted they counted 142.0 mg/L. They need to fall below 8.1 mg/L before I'm allowed to leave.

The liver creates this protein when there is inflammation in the body. The constant infusions of steroids have been soothing my body, washing through it. Every few hours the bags are changed; I sleep in short segments, polyphasic punctuation, and am woken several times a night by a whispering nurse, startled by the bright hallway, the motion, the artificiality. Like me, the nurses have had their sleep disturbed.

Outside I know there are small beings who remember their old ways and nevertheless navigate their new ones. The loss of habitat. The blue LED lights. The noise. Parking lots.

New encounters with the internal
the surprise of symptom
after the medication my insides
the blood the black-red evacuating

a leaf washes down and brushes
against the banks of my stony
gut bounding the rapids gentle
the broad blade of vegetation
drawing blood from the silt

I am forbidden fibre no more
flowers or stalks but certain
roots plucked from the cloched
darkness and boiled down
until you push and they grit the thumb

And then, at last, it is my last day. After a week of steroids, my C-reactive protein levels drop to 6.0 mg/L.

I watch the catheter drag from my vein and apply pressure to the cotton ball covering the hole, the bead of blood. It is a pinprick in reverse. I feel the sensation through the nerves of my molars, the sides of my tongue, the back of my throat as though I am gagging on relief.

I tremble as I walk from the ward. I get lost. Having been wheeled up to the top floor, I have no way of retracing my steps back down to the surface of the soil. From the open pedway I can see all the way down and lean my weak body over from the waist, looking past the white metal beams that cross floor to floor. I follow the light, my racing animal heart, and lift myself back up. Already I want to rest. I carry myself as fast as my weak, unused body will let me, recalling the sensation of walking more than a few feet at a time.

Almost nervous to cross the threshold, to go back outside. The bright winter, the cold, the air. The skin on my face is tight. The visual evidence of time: people move, traffic lights turn, snow falls. I am back again in the shocking urgency of the outside, the embrace of its volume and colour, feeling oddly unequipped to reintegrate. I call a car and nearly fall asleep on the ten-minute drive back home.

frozen scar, so hard shovel and seed resist, the flora

        On the other side I grow
interested in sites

        of various decay
bogs peatland muskeg

        where life in its varied scales
is nurtured

        alongside decomposition
where life breaks

        down and flourishes
in concert I am interested

in living
        in the muck I am interested

in the places
        where death feeds

endurance I am interested
        in where I am.

The land and I seem roughly
distressed best seen through
photographs to the moraines
on the other side along the edges
animals live along my edges
their fur coming off in my hands.

The boundary between
the shaggy sky and swelling
land a wet hairline the skinline
frothing the earth's foaming bovine
muzzle turned up above
the surrounding flesh of the land
rocking falling into its reputation
for swallowing living things whole.

Animate over the prairie bogs
are ambling formidable alliances brownswells
spreading over adjoining herds wet
kissing snout to snout absorbing pools
and seasonal separation into new families
this requires a proper send-off gifts
preserves a pouch for the medicine the sack
of the stomach the peat-dark pelt
against the rain the featherbed
blanket mire.

White delicate powder dusting
leaves on both sides

sporing insidiously and settling
in the crannies of the root systems

the fruiting bodies steam and wither
their networks falter from the iron

salt I swallow language
rots from the bottom up

what I repress can only be
image body preserved in flat blue.

It has jumped
from bark to bone its chroma
blossoming rosettes

from the shoulder to the elbow tissues

ringing it so rarely grows
on bone but yours
are so empty and inviting

Back at my window looking out, the river still glazed over in white. Underneath that white the river has grown hard.

My days now are ordered around numbers. I am always counting. I struggle against measurement and weight taking. I count out pills, calculate dosages, degrees. 40 mg of prednisone a day—eight tablets—for a week, then reduce by 5 mg each week. The long taper. Every day, 500 mg of metronidazole. I mark time, making sure I swallow down the prednisone before 9 a.m., take it with food, with 100 mg of azathioprine and two hours later the ciprofloxacin.

In the haze I am dreaming on the sharp banks of the river. Soil mites kiss my eyes. The masked ermine bounds in its white coat.

The introduction of calcium tablets so the steroids don't weaken my bones beyond what is considered acceptable given the goals of treatment.

A lone coyote dances in a ring, its youth yapping around my swollen self, woven within the mycelial strands and black humus and bloated bubbling opiates.

      I'm no enemy of the natural world only
of those who adulterate it

      I am home with the blue cattle
the mustard the toasted wood

      of the long low house where I am
lined with the winter wheat

      sheaving I am covered by the clement
eyes they visit

      upon me a gentleness I keep
from myself they share

      their forages grind in their velvet
mouths the yellow the green

      they carried from the end
of the season in worse days they were fed

      the plastic blown into their trusting
world from ours scraping

      their living tongues mounding inside
like a landfill a problem

        we made that their heavenly
hidden bodies must bear

        in the long cold of the long
room they nudge me on

        with their tufted snouts grazing
my fingertips for forgotten

        clover my own body turns in flaking
pain and shivers a cold

        sweat on the wind that they lick
away inside layers of oxen

        herding along the chambers
of their guts *Bos taurus* trampling

        the immortal plastic
into its component parts again

        as though their rumbling
hooves were enough to wind

        geological time back to its oils
and its waters the rumen

      microbiome dissolving human
error hubris reminding all domains

      of life that the natural world will
heal that winter is for resting

      that we can follow them in their slowness
close after their tolling bells.

When I arrive, I learn that the infusion clinic where I will be receiving doses of infliximab is composed of two small rooms on either side of a short hallway. On the right is one with three chairs and flimsy partitions between them that fail to conceal the reality of our exposure to one another. In the other, smaller room a single chair faces a row of filing cabinets and cupboards. Boxes of paper and other office supplies are piled in front of the cabinets and curve to fit the space at the side of the chair. I choose this room.

The second dose is set to take two hours to infuse and while I sit I hear others arriving and departing. Sometimes a nurse enters to rummage through a cabinet, contorting to avoid having to move the boxes in her way.

The pump at my side whirrs. The measured drip falls. I take a photo of myself amid the discards and excesses of health and care and their attendant bureaucracies.

Two hours after meals I swallow down the antibiotic that works by arresting the repair and replication of the bacteria inside me. Everything collapses from the inside. Hearing things that aren't there, feeling differently compromised.

Along the way these tablets invariably kill even those bacteria who are friendly, that tame stretches of my body into healthy terrain. Enough of them die and dysbiosis can set in, leaving you out of balance for as long as one year after treatment. Hurts me to help me.

Each day I swallow down 500 mg of ciprofloxacin, upon which the United States Food and Drug Administration has placed a "black box" warning for its potentially disabling side effects.[17] In Alberta patients are warned that quinolone antibiotics such as this "may cause serious and possibly permanent tendon damage (such as tendonitis, tendon rupture), nerve problems in the arms and legs (peripheral neuropathy), and nervous system problems," particularly prominent in those patients also treated with corticosteroids, as I have been.[18]

---

[17] Janice Hopkins Tanne, "FDA Adds 'Black Box' Warning Label to Fluoroquinolone Antibiotics," *BMJ* 337, no. 7662 (2008).
[18] "Ciprofloxacin—Oral," MyHealth Alberta, revised August 2024, https://myhealth.alberta.ca/health/medications/pages/conditions.aspx?Hwid=fdb0093.

Hold the permafrost to the landscape
like a painting a slab of mountain
a rash of biomass housed in crystal
suspension forced through
the meal into a net
of raised mineral
mounds all over the skin
that no one traverses
their little bodies on the roadside.

Swallowing the azathioprine, a doubled dose, now two chanterelles in the yellow and the diminutive. Slipping gender off, invisible. Two small spores in my palm that I swallow in the mornings.

To *suppress* is to "reduce (a person, a community, corporate body, etc.) to impotence or inactivity; to deprive of position or power; to keep in a state of subjection."[19] The daily consumption of these pills that settle in my gut and redirect its available pathways, trickling.

One of the most significant risks while on immunosuppressant medication is that of infection. Other things can burrow in and reside.

As in a bog, we look over the surface so as not to see the strata of our own dead we live atop. A perverse outpost on chill waters.

---

19 *Oxford English Dictionary*, "suppress (v.), sense 1a," accessed November 16, 2024, https://doi.org/10.1093/OED/1087179189.

The Scotch moss, the long daily lines
of tablets, the prednisone discs, white blossoms

                of moss that wet the path
                away from emergency that carry

my lightness my frame from borrowed hospital bed
back to my own where I can touch

                desire without being tethered to it to machine
                and monitor that knows when my heart

races and stops and calls
for someone in its ordinary voice

                from its real life to stop
                the fantasy that is meant to be

a mystery the body
has already its own ways of knowing.

White spruce through the hair to lift
from the scalp the white hard evidence
of my inflamed attached body snow
on the dark fur of my coat from within

the density of trees dances
it is good to stay close
to the skin of the earth brushed by needles
to crawl with your little strength

through white spruce to comb and soften
I am looked after by the trees
their psoriatic skin home to rustling
little things their fur and wings blanketing

where I land staving
off the banishing cold in their shared
agreement that as a community of survivors
they have had to learn.

I am waiting at the pharmacy across the street from the hospital for the injection. The thin green and blue stripes of the carpet. My boots melt into them.

To replenish vitamin D we bypass the oral route and deliver straight into the muscle. The pharmacist jokes with me that this will make me big and strong, a fantasy I still hold to. The bandage he puts over my arm is bright with cartoon characters. The pharmacist tells me to wait a few minutes in case of a reaction; they'll keep a watchful eye. My dad texts me. All of this I know is manageable, the management of disease taking place iteratively and with guidance, and still I am overwhelmed by the fact that I have gotten older and can only care for myself, no one to scoop me up and let me lie against their shoulder. Recalling the sensation of bobbing weightless in the arms of someone caring, boots threatening to slip from the foot.

Once enough time has passed I step back out into the day. The bright winter afternoon turns me transparent.

The steroids thin the skin and the azathioprine photosensitizes it.[20] As the drug's sediment settles on your shore you are increasingly vulnerable to ultraviolet A radiation and are therefore at increased risk of basal cell and squamous cell skin cancer.

I relax into the psychosomatic. The sun produces a new sensation on my skin. There's an immediate prickling and my body's instinct is to pull away. I am seen too much.

20 Lucy Howard et al., "Azathioprine, Risk of Skin Cancer and Use of Photoprotection: A Cross-Sectional Survey of Patients with Inflammatory Bowel Disease and Gastroenterology Clinicians," *Clinical and Experimental Dermatology* 49, no. 8 (2024): 903–904.

I was in the cold of the meadow my breath
fruiting the air in patterns I hope
are consistent with textbook images
medicine and diagnosis and their
ambitions my breath fruiting
the air.

                            Vapour branches and seeds in arrangements
                            of water suspended and blown away to transpire
                            later for some bird to bathe in to be sucked
                            up a vine traces of steroid cellular memory
                            how hard I tried to be well.

Blood sugar so high
I collapse weighted
by the heaviest wettest parts
my brains
one in head one in gut
both trickling in their cycles
a little longer.

I am to be given what is called a rescue dose. My body doesn't seem to respond quickly enough. My inflammation markers are still too high and so I need to be rescued by an additional dose. *Rescue*'s transitive verb: "To deliver (a person) from evil, trouble, or harm, *esp.* to save (a person) *from* a dangerous or distressing situation."[21]

"The average price of one 100-mg vial of originator and biosimilar infliximab in Canada is CAD $999 and CAD $528, respectively, based on provincial formulary prices."[22]

On behalf of the provincial government, Alberta Blue Cross administers a Non-Group Coverage program for which there is a monthly premium. This coverage will begin three months after submitting my application, which I did from my hospital bed. In the interim, this medication is covered by an assistance plan through the drug manufacturer that they call a compassion program.

Beginning around 1340, *compassion* began to mean a "feeling of emotion, when a person is moved by the suffering or distress of another, and by the desire to relieve it; pity that inclines one to spare or to succour."[23]

---

21 *Oxford English Dictionary*, "rescue (v.), sense 2a," accessed November 22, 2024, https://doi.org/10.1093/OED/5983600151.
22 Naazish S. Bashir et al., "Infliximab Pricing in International Economic Evaluations in Inflammatory Bowel Disease to Inform Biologic and Biosimilar Access Policies: A Systematic Review," *MDM Policy & Practice* 8, no. 1 (2023).
23 *Oxford English Dictionary*, "compassion (n.), sense 2a," accessed November 23, 2024, https://doi.org/10.1093/OED/6715341301.

You are not guaranteed life. You may not even want it. You will have to pay for it according to a schedule and to your political geography. It will feel hopeful and it will feel futile. It will feel like a burden. You will have to communicate it, meaning you will have to resort to language, meaning you will be alone.

The winding architecture of the hand
and wrist hanging from the dorsal venous
arch it crumbles
distributes strain I remember
walking beneath it and hearing
a brook's jewelled noise against stone
somewhere underground deep
in my body where there is some
reservoir I must draw from so long
as I live in this temporary structure

I have no love for myself. The persistent irritation, swelling, and scarring of my gut has meant that I struggle to absorb and metabolize that which I need to keep me going. Every few weeks I return to the infusion clinic where my veins are again tethered to a pump, this time dripping heavy mud-red liquid into me.

More than the infliximab, the iron drains. My gut aches and I feel tired, heavy, sometimes like I've been hit.

Somewhere along the line the cannula begins to leak. The bandage around the catheter is wet and dripping onto the towel under my arm. Everything is blue except for the rash of blood.

Looking out to a place I can't reach
on foot until the snow comes

under me are the tall generations
of conifers whose generations don't go

so far back only as far
as the trampling things grow

undisturbed far away neglect
blossoms unexpected

richness the northern bog
violet reseeds its mauves

across the bare gut plain
over the horizon

that colours the receding evening's gaze
neither malign nor benign.

Sometimes I forget. I am still not in the habit. A dose cannot be life and death. Yesterday it wasn't until mid-afternoon that I noticed I'd missed one. I flirted with taking the pills anyway, their double yolks in my palm, before calling the pharmacist to confirm. She told me to wait until tomorrow and resume my usual dose but gently scolded me about the importance of staying on top of one's medication. I returned the bottle to the medicine cabinet. Hives formed along the top of my hand as though it'd been slapped.

Later, on a walk, a discarded amber bottle by the edge of the creek, its pharmacy label nearly rubbed off, the lid still on, life preserved inside.

Drawing near the hot sickly vapour
beast and machinery falter unjoined
and delicate the corduroy road
far away swept out in the distance

and sucked down by the vacuous
slurping hole of extraction the blare
of the white metal horses of Wabasca
whinnying on their way down

plant debris lacing around the reaching
necks being pulled toward the oil
they were so desperate to reach but first
must pass the long true black of humus

here all travel goes one way
swallowing the pills the marrow
even the vomit
so well preserved

Whenever I arrive to my infusion appointment there is at least one other young person there, seated and hooked up and scrolling on their phone. These clinics administer all sorts of infusions and injections, but I eavesdrop and often these young patients are receiving the same medication as I am.

A 1988 study found that rates of Crohn's disease in northern Alberta were higher in urban areas than rural ones, and at the time the "peak prevalence" of the disease was below age twenty-nine and that the prevalence of young women diagnosed was approximately twice that of young men.[24] As of 2023, evidence shows that an estimated 825 per 100,000 people in Canada are living with inflammatory bowel disease, a total that reaches over 320,000 people. This study notes that prevalence of inflammatory bowel disease is expected to rise by "2.4% per year such that 1.1% of the population, 470,000 Canadians, will live with IBD by 2035."[25]

A hot dry winter, its matchbox edge, its promise. In the mewl of the future's air. We know what's coming and so wait for it, politely, in our soft construction.

---

[24] B.R. Pinchbeck et al., "Inflammatory Bowel Disease in Northern Alberta. An Epidemiologic Study," *Journal of Clinical Gastroenterology* 10, no. 5 (1988): 505–15.
[25] Stephanie Coward et al., "The 2023 Impact of Inflammatory Bowel Disease in Canada: Epidemiology of IBD," *Journal of the Canadian Association of Gastroenterology* 6, suppl. 2 (2023): S9–S15.

The future falls off
the flat distance near now
like a cliff throw
your voice down it lands
nowhere my life is
shortened a mouse's tail severed
its small brown
proteins curling and plucked
by the syringe by its scruff.

Waking in the early hours of January
> the narrow month this year so warm

it dangles from the ceiling spikes
> off the pendants slicing

my senses awake what is the point
> of going on when it all ends sharp

needle through the fabric both sides
> thick with the crossing of decisions loose

now and worn when it all ends and could
> end so soon slicing through

this unhealthy winter carriage
> under the long dangling threads

of lodgepole and then alongside
> them felled black-billed

magpies hop from one death
> to another trunks softening

under their lightness away
> from the city which with a single breath

can both love and destroy
> with its long glance and its evenness

life and death each side effect
    each doorway away from the city

the whites of the eyes flood with blown snow
    across the iris like cloth

upon which the red geometry
    of health is embroidered blood

unspooling from a loping mouth
    the terrain unrolling

like a micrograph a fatty liver
    white beads red.

the time it takes for the small mammals and uncommon
vegetables to live and die

and become the acres of fen that coil wetly inside
your temporary life

Another dose of azathioprine, duckling pair, its side effect of stomach pain reminding me that one needs to maintain a sense of humour when sick in a sick world.

Wetland is compromised, is brim filled to flowing, spills over in black oil, is altered, so when you fill a vial you see in its greater volume somehow a reduction of wetland, part by part. Is replaced in its degradation. Is not over. Is remembering: in childhood I knew the songs of loons, have not heard from them in a while. Is a mirror that catches more beneath the surface. Is not about seeing yourself. Is vulnerable. Is all over our hands. Is a feeling in the head after another dose that swells the face and your mind's aquatic processes. Seems unable to keep you alive although that, of course, is the point.

Sometimes the cut-up peat reveals
hidden bodies faces

                                      intact and smooth and graphite
                                      in some cases it's not just the skin

that remains internal
organs still looped on a walk

                                      on the banks where guts inflame
                                      more rapidly the garbage

in the river the smoke
in the sky from burning bodies

                                      our grey bodies are records
                                      shining like pencil pushed

too hard
it breaks.

Depression brought on by the loss
of glaciers and in the palm
opened by the earth a reservoir
to hold it water with yet more
pills floating in it brought to the mouth
down to the wet sphagnum mosses
of the gut a living system adjusted
acidic green starlike dying out
before you notice.

The brush line of pine in the years ahead
is then swept by the last mites below
my eyes like theirs milked over and drunk
cast down under wild moss and snow

we wind underneath the long-drying duff
that lifts fast like a boil on the skin
a somnambulism that hangs at the lip
and catches the lucky let in

the drowsy roots pour down the rocks to the dens
where the beetles make home in my bones
their hollows that horn with the lullaby blues
before flitting to sleep with the stones

the pale secret creature that cold in the night
moves from pillow and into my sleep
must drowsy and maudlin crawl into my warmth
and into my drugged dreams must weep.

An ecology icing over no chance
to taper off the drug dusting

the raw shaking body
how did I get by on so little?

My doses have increased as has the frequency with which I'm to receive them. Now I receive five vials every four weeks, 500 mg per month.

"The common maintenance schedule of infliximab for IBD is 5 mg/kg every 8 wk, irrespective of treatment with biosimilar or originator. This translates into approximately CAD $4,000 per dose for a 70-kg person. A regimen of 4 vials per dose costs CAD $26,000 per year with originator pricing and CAD $13,730 per year with biosimilar pricing."[26] At this rate, at minimum, my doses of biosimilar medication will cost $34,320 annually, divided between different insurance policies.

Still, the shadow of this amount follows me, worries me, makes it hard to heal.

---

26 Naazish S. Bashir et al., "Infliximab Pricing in International Economic Evaluations in Inflammatory Bowel Disease to Inform Biologic and Biosimilar Access Policies: A Systematic Review," *MDM Policy & Practice* 8, no. 1 (2023).

Dragging oneself like an animal shot out of the woods, the outside pink rolling out. At the kitchen table, head round and heavy, carried by the tide against my thoughts and away again. The water world: I suck down my pills, cranes fly low over the marsh, precious beads of water locked in plastic are forgotten. I make do with my own pain, my own small suffering, its scale a lash in the eye, an emergent tear.

Ice provided me with a way out
    out in the creek

               the snow erasing the permeability
        of states blanking everything holding

the little weight I have left
    my sleep keeps me

               from having to face the winter
sun I wake in the dead of night

my swollen moon
    face and I

        looking out
to our reflection in everything.

In another short life you are
a woman and then you are not out
of the rye the pickled mushrooms the sweet air
the plants of Siberian cedar rising like fur
on the animal walls your face rounds
like cupped hands holding water you swallow
fewer moons each day the long taper drip
slowly you drag the heavy tapestry off
your waxy endocrine system the warmth
reaches you from the past you fret
over the absurdity of living when she and you
and everyone else in this room are dead
days burn out days thrum to life
in another short life you see it through
herbs collecting in your gut
you are handed a handkerchief dry voices
crackle the first consonants of a folk song
somehow you just know the dance so you dance it
the room rises in emotion as you count out
the night together the snow outside
gathering at the window and peeking.

The red-backed vole skirting
its tunnels its cheeks
plump with lichen bounding
suddenly over the feet suddenly
you are lost

Stitching down the topsoil with icy threads
    all of it blown up by the changes in pressure

        when the iv drip begins it finds me cellular
    and stops me in my drifts the others here

kick up the dust lap with their thirsty tongues
    the water pulled from the stones under the swirling

        brown clouds they gather and organize they love
    and they strive against the ills

we dole out generously they take shape
    in ways I can never know this

        collective culture that has nothing
    to do with me.

I was in the hall waiting for the sun
to expire its long infirmity dimming the window

in the last of his light boxed and yellow are cut
nodding onions dripping their purple onto the dust

my daily dose has touched me left a bruise
where his bright hand falls my skin less

a barrier than material for his mark the genus
of paper flammable and dry the leaves

outside this room are brown and verbal
underpaw nocturnal appendages

carpet the outer world while here
all of our time is ringed

around itself the sun dies daily
the young coyote dashes

from the apartment's harsh bulbs
that will one day sprout underground

as will I if luck will let me I hope
then I can offer cover felted and invincible

to the shivering young of this changing place
while a yipping pack descends upon the river.

The big red fire comes vaulting over the mountain. The hills swollen and their lining of grass inflamed, the insects that turn the soil, the voles, its biome collapsing among the rush. The villi scythed. And you, your stems hollow like the fleeing waxwing, your lonely panicles waving in clusters. Your pneumatic veins heavy with scent.

Take this place a borderland
between the living and the dead hand
in glove.

                        The mire holds the boot.

I can't step out of this
dance based on the weight
of living and dead matter
within me I am prescribed
marbles yellow as innocence.

                        Basketed and glaucous I open
                          my furs to the abundant argyria
                        of her skin the surface under
                        which I and the other
                        fallen bodies hold
                        our breath among the cottonwood.

Where growth has been arrested wild
in miniature
through dark boreal lens the hermit thrust
its tail the only source of warmth red and nutty

brown-black spruce slender as the frame of a body
warbling on in its temporary footsteps
traversing this dangerous experience
on foot the unaccustomed trip

over the roots potted in the wide
container of land the uninitiated
in the etiquette of sickness to the logic
of balance step with the weight

of their health and notice too late the surface
collapsing the lining
of marsh flipping rearranging
capturing the body and swaddling it.

I continue the ascent, continue making my appointments, giving up my left hand to the needle, the drip bag, continue to look away from the puncture, the precise transgression of my body's boundary that would be so large if only I could see the way I want to.

mending in ways that draw attention to the wound

I hardly feel the effects anymore, which I take to mean everything is working as it should. I am gaining weight, the pain is less frequent and less intense. It can take months for the side effects to present in full but you can't borrow pain from the future. For now, it works until it doesn't.

The melt is starting. It is one of my favourite times of year: still cold enough to bite, menthol air deep in the lungs, and below, just underneath the thinning layer of ice, water snaking and bubbling, no origin point, starting everywhere.

This year has calmed me. I have accepted my boundaries. I have stayed quiet, lulled by this drip, this drip of spring, melt as medicine. I stand under it, shifting, the ground moving toward this new year, down toward the swallowing river.

MR ENTEROGRAPHY-GNH

Date: Mar 25, 2024
Status: Final
Ordering Provider:
Patient Location: EDM Grey Nuns Community Hospital
Clinicians Copied:
Accession Number:

Name: Purcell, Jason
Date of Birth:
Sex:

When I return to the river woollen
and partly poisoned I notice

a line in us both that does
not freeze over instead

the raw emerald of the inner earth
turns under the crust spinning

its grinding rotation through
its wound I stand right

at the tear and watch
the hardened vein refuse

winter refuse dormancy the declining
land calls me into recognition this place

is my teacher threads of steam
lift and my own boreal veins

embroidered all over my body
like seams open to the medicine

the masked ermine dances
in cursive bounds the vixen coughs

at the earth and it scatters in the humid
caverns amid the roots by the banks

my pain burrows the river is deep
from either surface returning

to it and laying my cheek
upon its threshold

it is temporary already
I feel it ending the night

falling the blanket woven
with quills and needles falling

square over me in its sharp
geometry after all this chalking

my tongue with the dry drugged snow
plunging my hands into the sleepy

saline I feel my body
crawl out of its numb casing

from my animal maw
comes a low bark a stream

of vomit the silver gleam
of remedy spreading

over the snow I return
to my old self all emotion

unbodied a fox leaving
its fur in the shape

of its activity in suspended pursuit
of its prey my health

folded like clothing at the river's edge
the landscape of management

is a place to stop rest temporarily
the body holds our weight as long as it can.

ACKNOWLEDGMENTS

This book was written in amiskwacîwâskahikan, Treaty 6 territory, where I live just on the lip of the river valley, and whose water and flora and fauna have been teaching me lessons in reciprocity and interconnectedness, in visiting and in listening.

This book was written in various states of sickness and healing, from hospital rooms, my own bed, or my living room couch, and always under the care of a team of doctors, nurses, and other medical professionals working within Alberta Health Services who, despite the impossible conditions of an underfunded and therefore crumbling public health system, help me to move through sickness with dignity.

To everyone at Arsenal Pulp Press: Brian Lam, Robert Ballantyne, Cynara Geissler, Jazmin Welch, Catharine Chen, JC Cham, Erin Chan, and Alison Strobel. Thank you for welcoming me back home with this book. It is an honour to work with each of you and a dream come true to find home among the truly incredible community of writers you have published.

To Jordan Abel, who has been a steadfast and generous editor, teacher, and friend, and whose support helped me start again. Thank you.

To ryan fitzpatrick, for the conversations about writing and about this book that were so generative.

To Mathew Thomson, for the beauty of your cyanotypes and allowing one to be used as this book's cover. Your work captures precisely moments I want to hold on to.

To Emily Riddle, Travis Chi Wing Lau, and Tea Gerbeza, for your blurbs and for your own writing that inspires and spurs me on. Thank you.

To Lindsay Meissner, for the conversation that inspired this book, without which this project would never have been.

To my friends from Glass Bookshop / Magpie Books: Julie King-Yerex, Moriah Crocker, Makda Mulatu, Zachary Ayotte, Arden Phillips, Rick

MacDonnell. Through the most difficult years, you've loved and carried me so that I could keep going. I am so thankful that I get to live this life with you all.

To my Edmonton family: Marie Carrière, Michelle Campos Castillo, Keighlagh Donovan, Sarah Drohan, Rhiannon Duval, Emily Hoven, Jessica Johns, Kyle Muzyka, Delainey Neddow, Kaitlyn Purcell, Kelsey Purcell, Emily Riddle, Eric Sirockman, Evan Skutle, Matthew Ward, Karyn Wisselink. You make this place home.

To my friends: Stephanie Blais, Natalie Amber Boustead, Shane Breau, Chelsea Butler, Kiona Callihoo Ligtvoet, Chelsey Campbell, Hilary Caplan, Brett Dahl, Jeremy Elder, Laura Jane Gladman, Mackenzie Ground, Marc-Olivier Hamelin, Shaun Hansen, Jim Johnstone, Derrick Jones, Justin Jones, Conor Kerr, Marcelle Kosman, Sarah Krotz, Cheyenne Rain LeGrande, Veronica Litt, Jacob Marchel, Hannah McGregor, Liam Monaghan, Juliana Montoya, Alex Mortensen, Patrick Nickleson, Alex Nierenhausen, Madelin Ogilvie, Kyla Pascal, Jon Pettigrew, Renée Poffley, Matt Remley, James Resendes, Mychaela Risling, Michelle Schultz, Vivek Shraya, Jay Smith, Kristine Smitka, Stephen Smolski, Ryan Spotowski, Bailey Sutton, Meghan Sych, Kyle Terrence, Mathew Thomson, Adam Topilko, Robbie Townsend, Iliana Turner, Simon Underwood, Julianna Wagar, Cameron Waller, Joshua Whitehead, Erin Wunker, Tatiana Zagorac.

To Justin Bilinski, for everything, with such abundance that words fail.

To the Alberta Foundation for the Arts and the Canada Council for the Arts, for their support of this project.

Photo credit: Zachary Ayotte

JASON PURCELL is from amiskwacîwâskahikan, Treaty 6, (Edmonton, Alberta), where they are currently a PhD student in the Department of English and Film Studies at the University of Alberta. They are the author of *Swollening* and *Crohnic*.

Colophon

This book has been typeset in Warnock Pro and Acumin Pro, both designed by Robert Slimbach.

Warnock Pro is a classic yet contemporary composition family named after John Warnock, the co-founder of Adobe Systems, whose visionary spirit has led to major advances in desktop publishing and graphic arts software.

Acumin is a versatile neo-grotesque sans-serif typeface family intended for a balanced and rational quality.